The ABCs
of Life

Journaling Your Way to Meaning

Carol Giacomucci

The ABCs of Life: Journaling Your Way to Meaning

Copyright © 2024 Carol Giacomucci. All rights reserved. No part of this book may be reproduced or retransmitted in any form or by any means without the written permission of the publisher.

Published by Wheatmark®
2030 East Speedway Boulevard, Suite 106
Tucson, Arizona 85719 USA
www.wheatmark.com

ISBN: 979-8-88747-184-6 (paperback)
ISBN: 979-8-88747-185-3 (ebook)
LCCN: 2024902127

Bulk ordering discounts are available through Wheatmark, Inc. For more information, email orders@wheatmark.com or call 1-888-934-0888.

rev202401

For my greatest teachers:

My parents,
My mother's faith in God and her undying patience.
My father's sense of humor and his work ethic.

My husband,
For his calmness and love.

My family and friends,
For their friendship and support.

My students,
For all the lessons I have learned from you.
It has been my greatest joy and privilege
to have been your teacher.

Foreword

As I begin this book, I am nearing retirement and thinking of all the lessons I've learned to bring me to this moment. Teaching for over thirty years, working with students in all levels of readiness and of all ages—from kindergarteners to older adults—I have learned more from my students about the human spirit than I could ever teach them about fluency and comprehension. I would like to use my experience as a teacher to help guide people who are struggling with their own situations; there is nothing greater than the human spirit and the desire to achieve lifetime goals. I also believe that writing is cathartic and assists us in resolving issues. Students come to school, balancing the entire weight of the world on their shoulders. So many have personal struggles with drugs, violence, and family situations. Schools have become social-work facilities, triaging students as they walk through the door—those students who are able to make it to school.

My choice of quotes in this book are purposeful. They are the same quotes that have helped me to navigate through challenging times in my life. My hope is that my students find their gifts or passions and find a way to make the world a better place. I want them to seek role models, ask for help when they need it, and try their best every day to live to their full potential. I want them to take pride in what they do, take responsibility for their actions, and be true to themselves.

This book is set up by the letters of the alphabet, each identifying a virtue along with a quote, allowing the reader to reflect and then to write a response.

Attitude

Your attitude is everything. Sometimes we miss out on the best things in life with the wrong attitude. It is very important to look at the positives of every situation. In the book, *How to Stop Worrying and Start Living* by Dale Carnegie, Carnegie states that if you are worried about something or are in a situation, think about the worst thing that could happen. If you can live with that, then stop worrying about it. I started to change the way I looked at what I thought was a bad situation, and I realized Carnegie was right. For example, one time I was flying from Phoenix to Santa Barbara, and I had to change planes twice. The original flight had a mechanical problem. We boarded the second plane, and the pilot told us that it, too, had a mechanical issue. Finally, the third airplane was functional, and we were only delayed for an hour and a half. The moment I heard the pilot explain the problem I, like others, became annoyed and upset. But then, I thought, what is the worst thing that can happen? We are delayed, or we don't fly that day. As soon as I processed the possible outcomes or consequences, I was no longer upset. I just realized that yes, that would be a problem to have to return the next day, however the probability of that happening was slim. Luckily, it was a short delay. So, the concept of just thinking of the worst scenario does help. It changes your mood—your perspective—and allows other people to enjoy your company rather than always perceiving you as uptight and anxious.

Facing life's challenges with a positive attitude will greatly affect the outcome of situations. According to John Hopkins Medicine, " ...people who are more positive may be better protected against the inflammatory damage of stress. Studies also find that negative emotions can weaken the immune response."
(Hopkins Medine.org)

What is your self-talk when you are feeling stuck or in a bad place?

____

____

____

____

____

____

____

____

B

Believe

"Believe you can, and you are halfway there."
—Theodore Roosevelt

Once you write down your goals, plan on how to attain those goals. You should be continuously moving towards your goals and adjust along the way.

"The privilege of a lifetime is to become who you truly are."
—C. G. Jung

"For I know the plans I have for you declares the Lord, plans for peace, and not for evil, to give you hope and a future."
—Jeremiah 29:11

"Sometimes God takes you on a journey you didn't know you needed to bring you everything you ever wanted. Trust the plan."
—Unknown

"You glow differently when your confidence is fueled by belief in yourself instead of validation from others."
—Ozge Mc Aree

"A bird sitting in a tree is never afraid of the branch breaking because her trust is not on the branch but on its own wings. Always believe in yourself." (themindsjournal.com)

What are your strengths?

____

____

____

____

What obstacles are you currently facing and how are they getting in your way of moving forward?

____

____

____

____

What can you do to resolve these obstacles?

____

____

____

____

Compassion

"People may not remember what you said to them, but they will remember how you made them feel."
—Maya Angelou

"Think for yourself, or others will think for you without thinking of you."
—Henry David Thoreau

If you are feeling lost, disappointed, or you just don't know what your next step is going to be, find a way to help others, even in the smallest of ways; you will then feel more grounded and able to focus. You never know the impact of even the smallest action and how it can help others. So, whenever you have the opportunity, do the right thing and help others. Pay it forward; it has a ripple effect on everyone around you.

Here are some examples of little ways you can help.

Feed a stray cat, help people in your neighborhood, create, and give out "Blessing Bags" to homeless in your community, drop off canned food items at your local food pantry or give them to someone in need, adopt a foster child around the holidays. The opportunities are limitless. Trust me, you will feel such an overwhelming sense of peace.

"Let no one ever come to you without leaving better and happier. Be the living expression of God's kindness. Kindness in your face, kindness in your eyes, kindness in your smile."
　　　　　—Mother Teresa

"The purpose of human life is to serve and to show compassion and the will to help others."
　　　　　—Albert Schweitzer

What are some ways you can help others?

____

____

____

____

____

After you help someone, explain how you feel.

____

____

____

____

D

Determination

Don't give up so easily. When you get frustrated by a task, just stop and take a break for a few minutes. Get a drink or take a quick walk and then come back to it. Most likely, you will find that you are able to quickly solve the problem. If you need assistance, ask for help. Divide the task into smaller parts. For example, if you must read a book for research or a report, count the total number of pages, then divide them into the number of days you will need to complete the task. Keep in mind that you will need time to write a summary of what you read each day. If you have a 250-page book, you have fifteen days to read. So, 250 divided by 15 equals 16.6 pages. If you need to organize your space via your backpack, office, closet, room, etc., start with one drawer or one section at a time. Take everything out, empty the space, and then sort through while making piles. One pile is for items to be discarded, the second pile is for items to be donated or recycled, and the third pile has the items you will keep. Organizing and uncluttering your space will make you feel better in all areas of your life.

Make Your Bed: Little Things That Can Change Your Life and Maybe the World by Admiral William H. McRaven is a great book to read. McRaven states ten principles that we can do to be successful. The first one starts with completing a task every day like making your bed. The title of the last chapter sums up the book—NEVER EVER QUIT!

Make a list of things you want to accomplish. What can you do every day to get closer to your goals?

____

____

____

____

____

____

____

____

____

____

Ego

Don't let your ego get in the way of yourself. It is always better to improve yourself. Don't belittle others when they are working on themselves too.

"The highest form of knowledge is empathy, for it requires us to suspend our ego and live in another's world."
—Plato

Sometimes we feel personally attacked by criticism from others. Instead of becoming defensive, let's try to become better by their words. For example, ask yourself: Is there any truth to what others are saying? How can I use their criticism to become stronger or better?

What are some things that you struggle with? Do you feel envious of others? Why do you think you feel this way? Are there qualities about yourself that you want to improve?

Faith

You must have a higher purpose or moral compass. Believe that you belong where you are right now and have the faith to know that you are here to make a difference in the world.

"It's funny how we outgrow what we once thought we couldn't live without, and then we fall in love with what we didn't even know we wanted. Life keeps leading us on journeys we would never go on if it were up to us. Don't be afraid. Have faith. Find the lessons, trust the journey."
—Mark and Angel Chernoff

"And we know in all things God works for the good of those who love him, who have been called according to his purpose."
—Romans 8:28

"Faith is taking the first step even when you don't see the whole staircase."
—Martin Luther King Jr.

"Faith is being sure of what we hope for, and certain of what we do not see."

—Hebrews 11:1

"There's no cloud too dark for God's light to penetrate if you keep on believing and have faith enough to wait."

—Unknown

What are your beliefs? Do you believe in God?

____

____

____

____

____

____

____

____

____

____

____

Gratitude

When you wake up every day, be thankful for the things you have. Every night before you go to bed, show gratitude for all you have been given.
"If you are not thankful for what you have, you will never be happy with getting more."
—Oprah Winfrey

When I was teaching in a women's prison, I remember an inmate who was working for me as a tutor. She was explaining to another inmate that regardless of your circumstances, there is always something to be thankful for. Even in the worst of situations, there is always a reason to be grateful.

"No man ever steps in the same river twice. For it's not the same and he's not the same man."
—Heraclitus

"Sometimes we don't realize the blessings we have until we no longer have them. Appreciate all the blessings in your life; take none for granted."
—Catherine Pulsifer

"Some people could be given an entire field of roses and only see the thorns in it. Others could be given a single weed and only see the wildflower in it. Perception is the key component to gratitude, and gratitude a key component to joy."
—Amy Weatherly

"I complained I had no shoes until I saw a man with no feet."
—Shakespeare

"Gratitude helps us to see what is there instead of what isn't."
—Annette Bridges

"Someday you'll be grateful God gave you what you needed instead of what you wanted."
—Jam Alker

"Gratitude helps you fall in love with the life you already have."
—Kristen Hewitt

Make a list of all your blessings and what you are grateful for

____

____

____

____

____

Hopefully, you will see that most of these can't be purchased with money.

H
Happiness

"Don't allow others to hold your happiness in their hands, hold it in yours so it is always within your reach."
—Unknown

Live your life for yourself. Don't try to please other people.

"If you want to feel rich, count all the gifts you have that money can't buy."
—Picture Quotes.Com

"Happiness cannot be traveled to, owned, earned, worn, or consumed. Happiness is the spiritual experience of living every moment with love, grace, and gratitude."
—Denis Waitley/ MF Facets

"Ten years from now, make sure you can say that you chose your life, you didn't settle for it."
—Mandy Hale

"Rivers do not drink their own water; trees do not eat their own fruit; the sun does not shine on itself and flowers do not spread their fragrance for themselves. Living for others is a rule of nature. We are all born to help each other. No matter how difficult it is … life is good when you are happy; but much better when others are happy because of you."

—Pope Francis

Write down three things that bring you the greatest joy. Are they activities or relationships?

1.

____

____

____

2.

____

____

____

3.

____

____

____

Now, try to engage in these three things every day without omitting your other obligations.

I

Integrity

"Integrity is doing the right things when no one is looking."
—C. S. Lewis

It is never wrong to do the right thing. You will not have to look behind your back when you know you are making good choices.

"The lessons I want you learn is … it doesn't matter what you look like. You can be tall, short, or fat or thin or ugly or handsome like you Father, or you can be black or yellow or white, it doesn't matter. What does matter is the size of your heart and the strength of your character."
—Herman Munster

In the book, *The Fred Factor* by Mark Sanborn, Fred is a mail carrier that goes to great lengths to provide his customers with the best customer service. If everyone had Fred's core values and desire to help others, the world would be a better place. This book is an excellent read and you will walk away with a greater sense of purpose.

"If it's not true, don't say it. If it's not right, don't do it."
—Marcus Aurelius

"You cannot get through a single day without having an impact on the world around you. What you do makes a difference, and you have to decide what kind of difference you want to make."
—Jane Goodall

The Woman and the Hunchback
by Madhu Chanda Das-Krishan

Once there was a woman who baked bread for her family and another loaf for a hungry passerby. She kept the extra loaf on her windowsill. Every day a hunchback came and took the bread. Instead of thanking the woman, he would say, "The evil you do remains with you; the good you do comes back to you." Soon the woman became annoyed. "He is never thankful," she thought. "He only repeats the same words."

One day, she decided to put an end to him. She added poison to the extra loaf. As she was about to put it on the windowsill, she stopped and thought to herself, "what am I doing?" She then threw the poisoned loaf away and quickly baked a fresh loaf and put it on the windowsill. Within some time, the hunchback came and took the loaf from the windowsill and muttered: "The evil you do remains with you; the good you do comes back to you!" Then he left, not knowing how upset it made the woman.

One day, as the woman placed the loaf on the windowsill, she prayed for her son's safe return. He had been traveling for months and she had not heard from him. That night, there was a knock on the door and as she opened it, she saw her son, who had grown thin, his clothes were dirty and torn. He said, "Mother it is a miracle I am alive. I was about a mile or so away and so very hungry that I collapsed. I was sure to perish, but then a hunchback passed by, and I begged him for some food. He was so kind to me; he gave me an entire loaf of bread. As he gave it to me, he said, "This is what I eat every day. It looks as though you need it more that I." Hearing those words, the woman became pale. She realized, had she not thrown the poisoned loaf away, her son would have eaten it and surely perished. She then realized the significance of the hunchback's words. "The evil you do remains with you; the good you do comes back to you!"

Moral: Do good and don't ever stop doing good deeds, even if you don't feel appreciated because some day you will be rewarded for your actions.

Explain about the times when your integrity has been challenged?

____

____

____

____

____

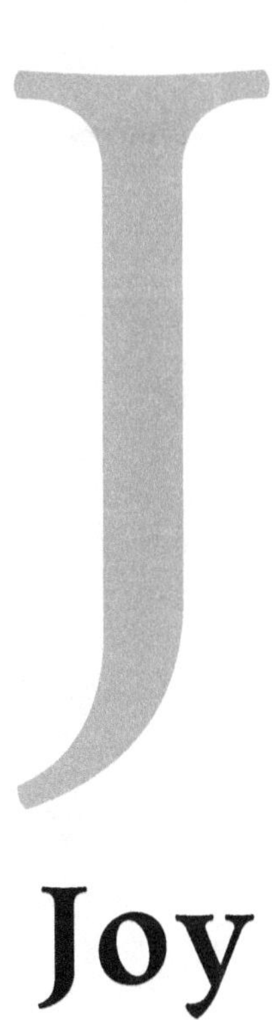

Joy

I believe joy and peace go hand in hand and are equally important. In most situations, what brings you peace is usually your greatest joy. What gives you joy, brings you peace. Watching the sunset fills my heart with joy—just watching it, and at the same time, it gives me peace. I truly hope that you fill your life with both.

"Live your truth boldly."
—Ted Roberts

Others may decide to think less of you, but it isn't your job to prove your worth. Just keep moving forward doing what you believe is right for you.

"It's your job to live knowing your worth can never be defined by another's assumptions. You are strong, you are brave, you are worthy, you are enough. Hold your head high, be proud. Carry on."
—Rachel Marie Martin

What brings you the greatest joy?

K

Kindness

"Many years ago, I was fishing, and as I was reeling in the poor fish, I realized, I was killing him for the passing pleasure it brought me. And something inside me clicked. I realized as I watched him fight for breath, that his life was as important to him as mine was to me."

—Paul McCartney

"You may not always see the results of your kindness, but every bit of positive energy you contribute to the world makes it a better place for all of us."

—Lisa Currie

"Be thankful for the difficult people in your life, for they have shown you who you do not want to be."

—Unknown

One at a Time
Adapted from Loren Eiseley

A tourist was walking down a deserted beach at sunset. As he walked along, he began to see a man in the distance. As he grew nearer, he noticed that the man kept leaning down, picking something up and throwing it out into the water. Time and again he kept throwing things out into the ocean. As the tourist walked even closer, he noticed that the man was picking up starfish that had been washed up on the beach and, one at a time, he was throwing them back into the water. The tourist was puzzled. He approached the man and said, "Good evening, I was wondering what you are doing."

"I'm throwing these starfish back into the ocean. You see, it's low tide right now and all of these starfish have been washed up onto the shore. If I don't throw them back into the sea, they'll die up here from lack of oxygen."

"I understand," the tourist replied, "but there must be thousands of starfish on the beach, you can't possibly get all of them. There are simply too many. This is probably happening on hundreds of beaches up and down this coastline. Can't you see that you can't possibly make a difference?" The man smiled, bent down, and picked up yet another starfish. Then he threw it back into the sea and replied, "Made a difference to that one!"

So, you see, what you do makes a difference. Don't ever feel defeated when trying to help others or by being kind. Sometimes we don't see the positive effects of our actions until much later.

What acts of kindness have others done for you?

Love

"In a relationship, you shouldn't have to think five steps ahead, walk on eggshells, anticipate their mood, take the blame for all tensions, read their mind, apologize for their behavior, and fear they may stop loving you from one day to the next. This isn't healthy love, it is control."
—Emma Ro

"Love has nothing to do with what you are expecting to get—only with what you are expecting to give—which is everything."
—Katherine Hepburn

"Where there is love there is life."
—Mahatma Gandhi

"The greatest happiness of life is the conviction that we are loved; loved for ourselves; or rather, in spite of ourselves."
—Victor Hugo

"Never love anyone who treats you like you're ordinary."
—Oscar Wilde

"There is only one happiness in this life, to love and be loved."
—George Sand

"Love is always patient and kind. It is never jealous. Love is never boastful or conceited. It is never rude or selfish. It does not take offences and is not resentful. Love takes no pleasure in other people's sins but delights in the truth. It is always ready to excuse, to trust, to hope, and to endure whatever comes."
—1 Corinthians 13:4–7

Who are the people in your life that you cherish and why?

____

____

____

____

____

____

____

____

____

M

Manners

People will respect you when you demonstrate courtesy and good manners.

Holding the door for someone behind you, helping someone in need in a split second. Giving your seat to an older or disabled person. Smiling or saying hello to people as you pass them in a hallway, store—anywhere. Having manners will get you further in life. I believe now more than ever our society lacks this social norm. People are more involved in using their personal devices than in being in the moment and giving their time to others. My wish is for people to interact more with those around them, than to be engrossed with social media. Be present and give your full attention to the person you are with.

"You're not a grown up until you know how to communicate, apologize, be truthful, and accept accountability without blaming someone else."

—Unknown

"Manners are the social norms and customs that guide how we interact with others in society. They are important because they help us communicate respect, kindness, and consideration for others, and they facilitate positive social interactions."
—Gaurav Kushwaha

The Golden Rule: "Do unto others as you would have them do unto you."
—Jesus in His Sermon on the Mount

What can you do to improve your manners, your interactions with others?

____

____

____

____

____

____

____

____

____

Nourish

Nourish, according to Webster's dictionary, means to provide with the food or other substance necessary for growth, health, and good condition. It is important to keep learning and growing in all areas of life. Learning something new keeps your brain cells growing and provides contentment for your spirit and your soul. I love to wander through my local library to find books and classes on interesting topics.

"The mind that opens up to a new idea never returns to its original size."

—Albert Einstein

"Surrounding yourself with good people can affect every aspect of your life, from business to romantic relationships. When you surround yourself with positivity, you're more likely to adopt empowering beliefs and see life as happening for you instead of to you."

—Tony Robbins

What ways do you "nourish" your body, soul, spirit, and mind?

Opportunities

"Each place along the way is somewhere you had to be in order to be here."

—Wayne Dyer

"You can't go back and change the beginning, but you can start where you are and change the ending."

—C. S. Lewis

"If you are not willing to work for it, don't complain about not having it."

—Toby McKuken

"A positive mind finds opportunity in everything. A negative mind finds fault in everything."

—Unknown

"Often, when you think you are at the end of something, you're at the beginning of something else."

—Fred Rogers

"Don't let your bubble burst just because your dream hasn't come true yet. Your dreams are worth waiting for."
—Carol CC Miller

"Life is an opportunity; benefit from it."
—Mother Teresa

What opportunities do you have? How can you create better opportunities?

____

____

____

____

____

____

____

____

____

____

P

Peace

I think having peace is the most important feeling one can have. It's a knowing that you did everything you could do in a given situation. It is just like playing a sport. If you lose the game, you can lose with a sense of peace if you played your best. Never be ashamed of losing anything so long as you know that you tried your best.

"The moment you accept responsibility for everything in your life is the moment you gain the power to change anything in your life."
>—Hal Elrod

"I believe that everything happens for a reason. People change so that you can learn to let go. Things go wrong so that you appreciate them when they are right, and sometimes good things fall apart so that better things can fall together."
>—Kevin Gates

"You are not obligated to sacrifice your peace for those who aren't at peace with themselves."
>—Imterencelester

"A positive mind finds opportunity in everything. A negative mind finds fault in everything."
—Unknown

"The longer you entertain what's not for you, the longer you postpone what is. Read that again."
—TrulyKaykay-Twitter

"Control how you respond to things sent to destroy your peace."
—Unknown

"Best career advice I can give: Don't ever attach yourself to a person, a place, a company, an organization, or a project. Attach yourself to a mission, a calling, a purpose ONLY. That's how you keep your power and your peace."
—Erica Williams Simon

When my first love and I went our separate ways, I was completely devastated. It was the saddest I had ever felt. While I was sitting on a bench wallowing in self-pity, I heard a peculiar sound. The sidewalk had a slight incline, so I couldn't see below the hill. The sound was getting closer and closer. Finally, I saw a man in a wheelchair, sweat flowing down the side of his temple, slowly turning the wheels of his chair as it hit the cracks in the sidewalk.

I immediately got mad at myself. Here I was, upset over a relationship when this young man was struggling in his chair just to get somewhere independently. I realized that there will always be someone whose circumstances are far more challenging than my own. I learned to be grateful for the experience, grieve for the loss, make peace with myself, and move forward with my life. There is always a lesson to be learned from everything we go through—even when those experiences are painful. But if we have the right perspective, the best is yet to come.

The Cross Room

A young man was at the end of his rope. Seeing no way out he dropped to his knees in prayer, "Lord, I can't go on," he said. "I have too heavy a cross to bear." The Lord replied, "My son, if you can't bear its weight, just place the cross inside this room. Then open that other door and pick out any cross you wish." The young man was filled with relief. "Thank you, Lord," he sighed, and he did what he was told. Upon entering the other door, he saw many other crosses, some so large the tops were invisible. Then he spotted a tiny cross leaning against the far wall. "I'd like that one Lord," he whispered. And the Lord replied, "My son, that is the cross you just brought in."
—Unknown

What brings you peace?

____

____

____

____

Quiet

"Much is accomplished in the pauses of life. God renews our strength in those waiting times."
—Isaiah 40:31

Whenever I have a big decision to make or I just feel out of sorts, I take a walk or find a quiet place away from people. I can sit and be still while thinking about the outcomes, or just pray. Usually, the solution reveals itself. If you can just sit in nature or be still, there is a calm that can uplift you.

"Everyone needs a place to retreat, a spot where the world grows quiet enough for the soul to speak."
—Angie Weiland-Crosby

"Stillness provides an opportunity to observe our frenetic thoughts, tune into our bodies, and listen to what life is trying to tell us. It helps to reduce stress, improves sleep and listening, provides new ideas, and reminds us of the present moment."
—Beverly D. Flaxington, *Psychology Today*

Where do you go to be still and think?

82

R

Relationships/
Respect

Life is all about relationships. You can't get through this life without having relationships. I think God puts the right people in your life for a reason. I don't believe in coincidences. Sometimes, you are someone else's answer to prayer, so it is important to help everyone who comes across your path. It goes back to holding the door open for others, being kind, smiling, saying good morning. What you put out in the world comes right back to you.

"Your life will be appreciated by the right people; it is up to you to know who they are. Your time and energy are an investment into the lives that show it in return. Be there for those who are there for you—that's it, end of story."
—J. M. Preston

"Show respect to people who don't even deserve it; not as a reflection of their character, but as a reflection of yours."
—Dave Willis

"Remove yourself from anywhere you don't feel valued, appreciated, or respected."
—Natalie Wills

In Mark Sanborn's book, *The Fred Factor*, Fred, Mark's mail carrier, always went above and beyond to help his customers. He was more than just a mail carrier; he invested in his customers' lives. "Where others might have seen delivering mail as monotonous drudgery, Fred saw it as an opportunity to make the lives of his customers more enjoyable. He chose to make a positive difference."
—Mark Sanborn, *The Fred Factor*, page 9

Sometimes, just the smallest of gestures can make a big difference. You may not think your actions are significant, but they can have a positive effect on a person's day.

Write down three to five statements that you feel are your core attributes or values that are non-negotiable.

____

____

____

____

____

Skills/
Education

Your education and skill set are very important. Evaluating what you want to do with your life and improving your skills are necessary for success.

"Do the work today so that your future self has everything you've ever wanted. Trust the timing of your life and truly believe that the best is yet to come!"

—Unknown

Always be a lifelong learner. According to Emma Parkhurst in her article, "The Benefits of Being a Lifelong Learner," (August 1, 2022, Utah State University) lifelong learning increases your self-esteem and confidence along with your cognition and memory. Creating social connections "can develop new relationships." Many people also "feel better about themselves and they have a greater ability to cope with stress, as well as a greater sense of hope and purpose."

My mother had seven children; I am the youngest. When I was ten years old, she was forty-five and decided to return to school to get her GED. Then she attended nursing school and became a licensed practical nurse. She never let her age or her circumstances alter her goals. An education, at any age, is never a waste of time.

What are your educational goals? In what ways do you want to increase your skills?

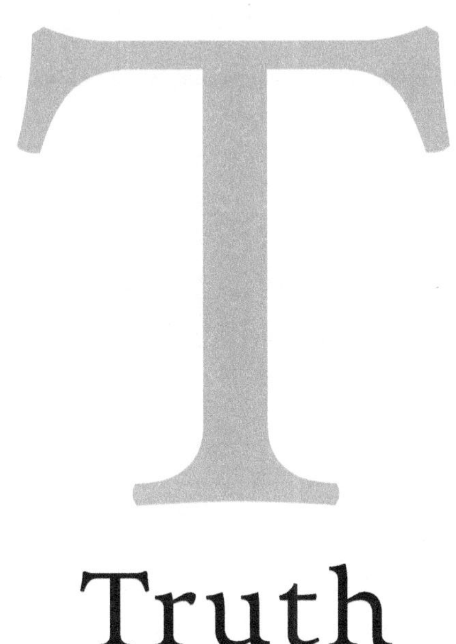

Truth

Aways seek the truth. Find the truth in everything you do, and speak only the truth regardless of the situation. *The Four Agreements: A Practical Guide to Personal Freedom* by Don Miguel Ruiz has four principles that explain, "One should always do their best, be impeccable with your words, don't take anything personally, and don't make assumptions." I highly recommend reading this book; it is a great reference and guide. "Dishonesty leads to more dishonesty and creates an energy around you that feels unsafe, unsure, and unclear. Break through this energy and speak your truth; it will always set you free."

I only surround myself with people who are honest, don't play games, and who value me. Once people get to know you, they will also realize that you are a person who seeks the truth and speaks the truth.

"A lie can travel halfway around the world while the truth is putting on its shoes."

—Mark Twain

What are your essential truths?

U

Unique/
Universe

"Surround yourself with people who reflect who you want to be and how you want to feel. Energy is contagious."

—Rachel Wolchin

Being true to yourself, having goals, and making a plan to achieve those goals will lead to a more purposeful life. Find your gifts and your passion. Then find a way to help those who are less fortunate, and make that your purpose. When you invest in others, it truly enriches your own life.

"She silently stepped out of the race she never wanted to be in. She found her own lane and proceeded to win."

—Unknown

"Ten years from now, make sure you can say that you chose your life; you didn't settle for it."

—Mandy Hale

"Each place along the way is somewhere you had to be in order to be here."

—Wayne Dyer

What makes you unique? What is your view of the universe?

Voice

Use your voice to make the world a better place. Speak up when you see something that you feel is wrong.

"An environment that is not safe to disagree is not an environment focused on growth; it's an environment focused on control."
—Wendi Jad

"One voice can change a room, and if one voice can change a room, then it can change a city, and if it can change a city, it can change a state, and if it can change a state, it can change a nation, and if can change a nation, it can change the world."
—Barak Obama

"There is no greater agony than bearing an untold story inside you."
—Maya Angelou

What is one way you want to use your voice to change something?

Worth and Wealth

"If you want to feel rich, just count all of the gifts you have that money can't buy."
—Unknown

"You should never feel like you have to convince someone of your worth. You matter; you are more than enough."
—Barb Schmidt

If you are not feeling valued by those around you, you need to find another place or other people who will respect and value you and accept you for who you are.

"Do the work today so that your future self has everything you've ever wanted. Trust the timing of your life and truly believe that the best is yet to come."
—Unknown

"You cannot get through a single day without having an impact on the world around you. What you do makes a difference, and you have to decide what kind of difference you want to make."
—Jane Goodall

One Thanksgiving, after returning to my car at the grocery store, I saw an elderly man staring at me through the passenger window. He wore glasses, and one eye was crusted over. His lip was quivering. He had white hair and looked to be in his mid seventies. He was wearing a dirty white dress shirt and what was probably one of his best slacks and dress jacket. My heart immediately sank. I got out of my car and told him that I didn't have any cash. I am sure he heard that story before. Before I could finish my sentence, he turned and slowly walked away. I felt horrible and wondered what I could do for him. The expression on his face remained with me as I ran my other errands.

After an hour, I went into McDonald's and, using my credit card, bought five hamburgers and placed each in their own bag. Then I went back to the parking lot where I last saw the elderly man. I drove around the area until I found him sitting on a bench at the bus stop with a few of his friends. I got out of my car and handed each of them a bag. The expression on their faces was priceless. It was the best five bucks I ever spent.

What is your definition of wealth?

____

____

____

____

Xenacious

(filled with a yearning for change)

Change is inevitable and can be a positive experience if we have the right attitude. Some examples of positive change include finding a new way of doing something and learning something new. Even taking a different route to work or school can be exciting. Experimenting with new food, clothes, games, books, etc. can also provide opportunities to grow. Change can open new ways of thinking.

Explain an area in your life that you feel you want to change?

____

____

____

____

____

____

____

112

You

You were born for a reason and purpose. "The only obligation in any lifetime is to be true to yourself."

"Don't compete with anyone else but be better than you were the day before and today."
>   —Cherokee wisdom

"Don't lose the spark that makes you ...you."
>   —C. J. Peterson

The Man and the Butterfly
>   — Author unknown

One day, a man found the cocoon of a butterfly. A small opening appeared, and he sat and watched the butterfly for several hours as it struggled to force its body through the little hole. Soon it seemed to stop making any progress. It looked as if it had got as far as it could, and it could go no farther. The man decided to help the butterfly. He took a pair of scissors and cut off the remaining part of cocoon. The butterfly then emerged easily. But it had a swollen body and small, shriveled wings. He continued to watch the butterfly because he thought that, at any moment, the wings would open and expand to be able to support the body, which would contract in time. This didn't happen! In fact, the butterfly spent the rest of its life crawling around with a swollen body and shriveled wings. It never was able to fly. What the man in his kindness and haste did not understand was that the restricting cocoon and the struggle required for the butterfly to get through the tiny opening were God's way of forcing the fluid from the body of the butterfly into its wings so that it would be ready for flight once it achieved its freedom from the cocoon.

Sometimes struggles are exactly what we need in our lives. If God allowed us to go through our lives without any obstacles, it would cripple us. We would not be as strong as what we could have been. We could never fly.

Explain a situation where you grew in character because of a struggle. In what ways did it change you?

____

____

____

____

____

____

Zeal

"Surround yourself with positive people who push you to do and be better. No drama or negativity. Just higher goals and higher motivation. Good times and positive energy. No jealousy or hate. Simply bring out the absolute best in each other."
—Unknown

"Surround yourself with people who reflect who you want to be and how you want to feel. Energy is contagious."
—Rachel Wolchin

"Your life will be appreciated by the right people. It is up to you to know who they are. Your time and energy are an investment into the lives that show it in return. Be there for those who are there for you. That's it, end of story."
—Jim Preston

Ride Your Own Ride

I have been an avid bicyclist for most of my life. In the mid-nineties, I rode with a bike club, and we were preparing for the

MS 150, which raises money for Multiple Sclerosis. We were also training for the Tour de Tucson. Since I had never ridden a national ride before, I had a lot of anxiety and questions. One day while on a training ride, I decided to ask a fellow club member all my questions. Herman Baer (1930–2022) was a tall, burly man in his mid-sixties with a full head of white hair. He was a former marine with a strong Boston accent, and I knew he would really "tell me like it is." So, one morning as we were riding, I started with my questions. "Do I stay with the pack? How long should I ride before stopping for a break?"

He shook his head and interrupted me before I could ask my next question. "No, no," he said. "When you have a tailwind, just put it in your big chain and ride. When you have a headwind or a hill, put it in your granny chain and put your head down and ride. Don't worry about what other people are doing. Just ride your own ride. When you feel like you need to stop, then stop. Who cares what other people are doing? That doesn't matter. Just ride your own ride."

I believe this advice correlates with how we should live our lives. You need to do what you feel is right for you, regardless of what others are doing. You need to do what you believe is the right thing for you and your life.

I hope that this book has offered you a new perspective and helped you open new paths and opportunities. I hope that you live a full, exciting, and purposeful life. Find your gifts/passion, then find a way to help the world. You were born for a reason and a purpose. The idea of "changing the world" begins with

changing how you think about things. If you change your perspective or the way you do things, it will have a ripple effect.
Make your goals and come up with a plan for how to attain those
goals. Write down the steps on how to attain those goals and
strive to reach them every day.

Most of all, I hope you "ride your own ride."